DISCARD

EASY-READ FACT BOOKS

Trees

Andrew Langley

Franklin Watts
London · New York · Sydney · Toronto

© 1987 Franklin Watts Ltd

Franklin Watts
12a Golden Square
London W1

First published in the USA by
Franklin Watts Inc.
387 Park Avenue South
New York, N.Y. 10016

Franklin Watts Australia
14 Mars Road
Lane Cove
NSW 2066

Phototypeset by Keyspools
Limited
Printed in Hong Kong

UK ISBN: 0 86313 631 1

US ISBN 0-531-10446-X
Library of Congress Catalog
Card No: 87-61350

Photographs:
David Jefferis
Frank W Lane

Illustrations:
James Dugdale
Eagle Artists
Hayward Art Group
Michael Roffe
David Salayia
Zefa

Design:
Janet King
David Jefferis

Technical Consultant:
Alan Mitchell BA, B.Agric.(For.)

Note: The majority of
illustrations in this book
originally appeared in "Trees"
An Easy Read Fact Book.

Contents

A world of trees	4
The parts of a tree	6
A look inside the trunk	8
Roots and branches	10
Leaves	12
Flowers and fruit	14
Sowing the seed	16
Seedlings	18
Life in a tree	20
How old is it?	22
Forestry	24
Fire!	26
The many uses of wood	28
Tree facts	30
Glossary	31
Index	32

A world of trees

Trees grow in almost every part of the world. Some grow well in dry places, others like damp conditions. Some grow on flat plains, others in hilly regions. The only areas where trees will not grow are deserts and very cold places.

Scots Pine · Oak

Sapling · Youth · Maturity · Windy place · Mea...

Forest

The size and shape of trees depend on how old they are and where they grow. Seen here are the stages in the growth of a Scots Pine and the shape of an Oak growing in different places.

The parts of a tree

Trees are like other plants, except that they are usually larger and woody. A large part of the tree grows under the ground. The roots draw up water. Above ground is the thick trunk. At the top are the branches and leaves. This upper part is called the crown.

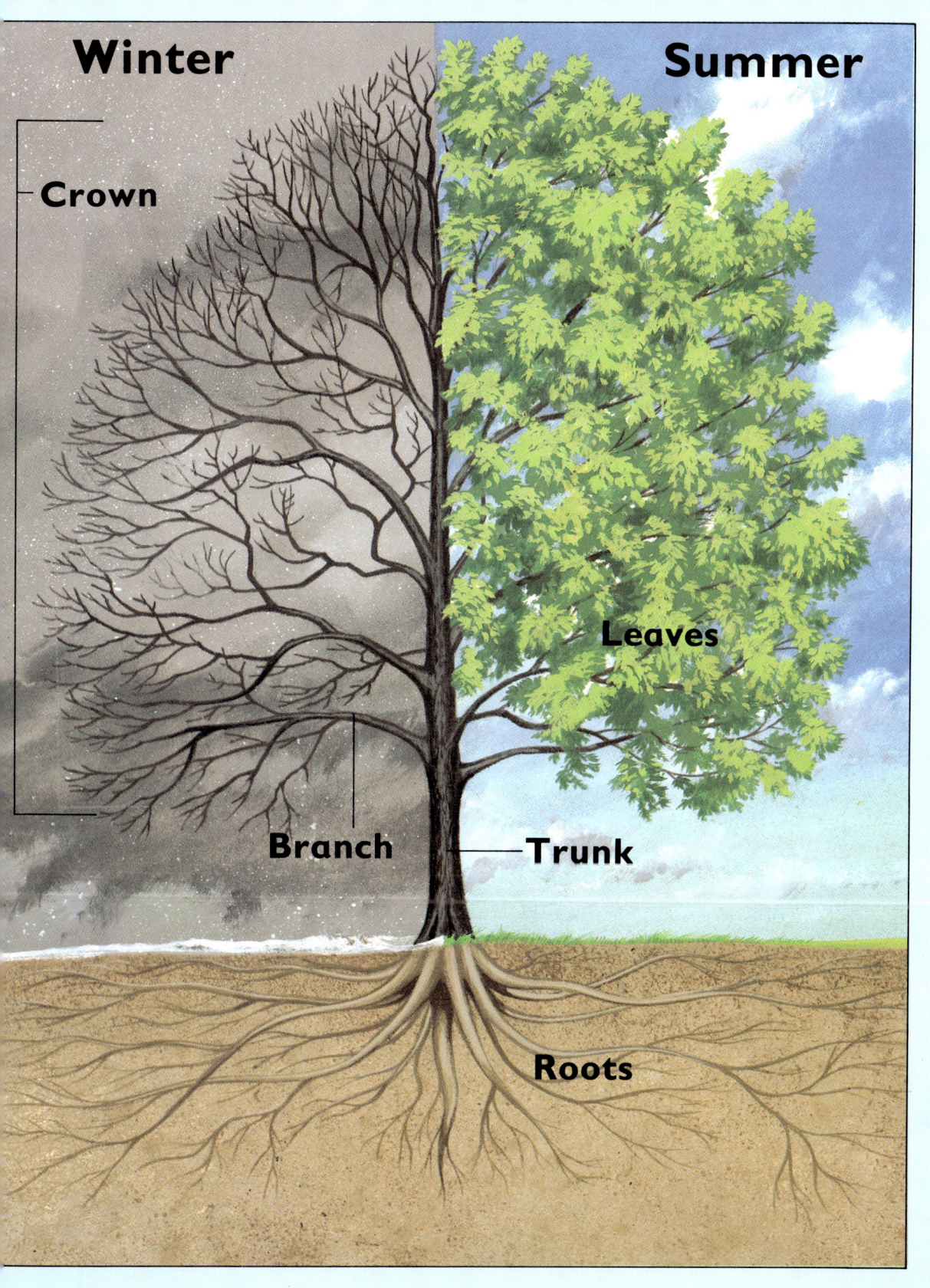

A look inside the trunk

Heartwood: The dead core of a tree.

Sapwood: Carries sap (water and minerals) from the roots to the leaves.

Cambrium: The part of the trunk that forms new growth.

Phloem: Carries food from the leaves to the branches, trunk and roots.

Bark: The tough skin which protects against attack from weather and animals.

A tree trunk has many layers. Most of a tree trunk is made of sapwood. This carries sap from the roots to the leaves. At the center of the trunk is the heartwood.

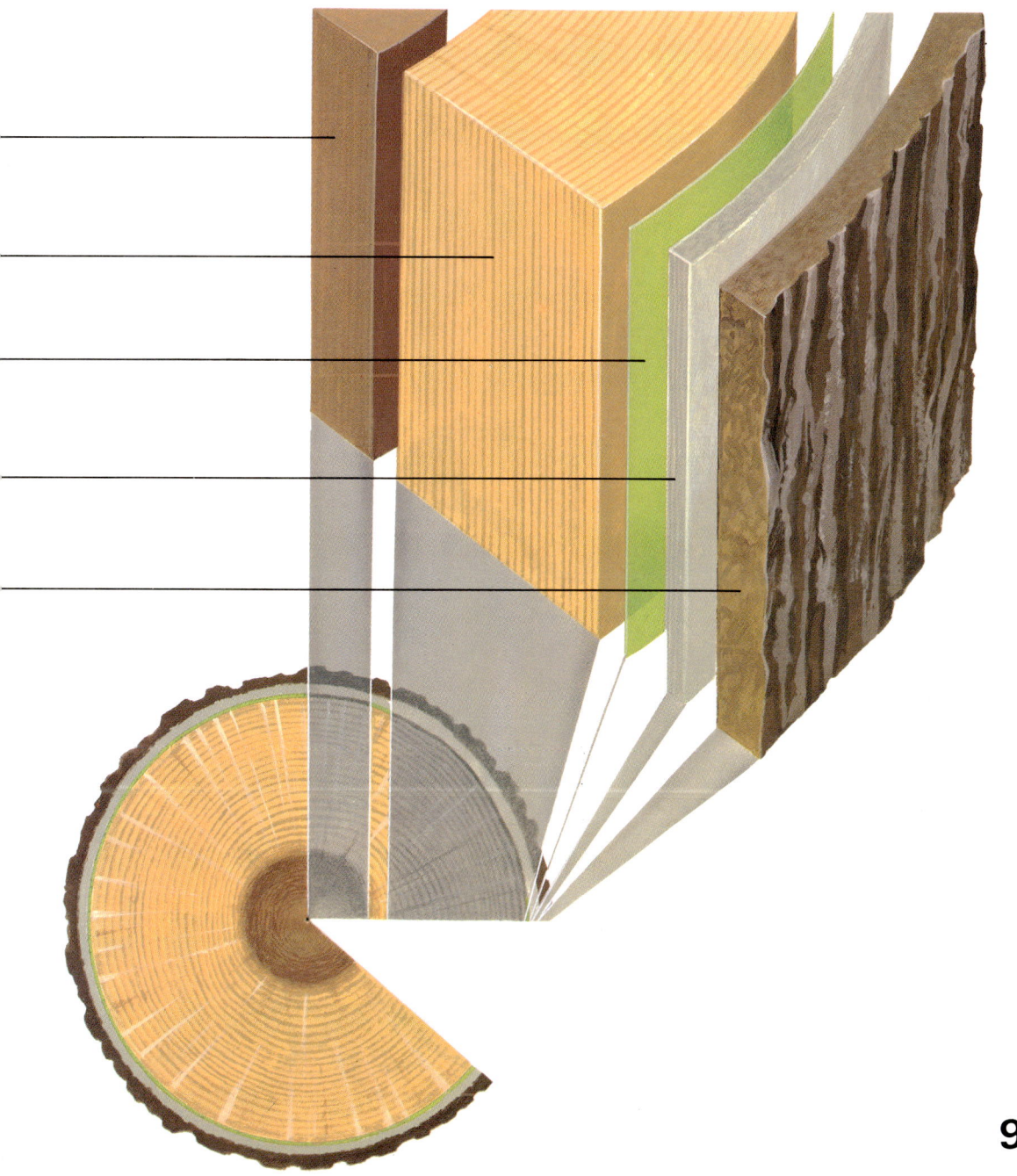

Roots and branches

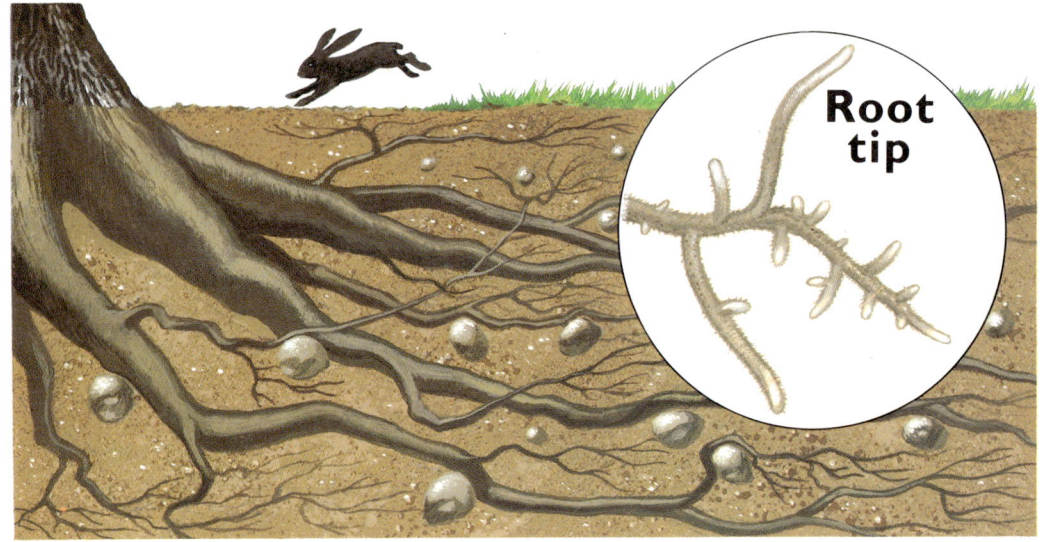

The roots spread out below the ground. Their tips are covered in tiny hairs. These take in water and minerals from the soil. The roots also hold the tree firm and upright in the ground.

A branch grows longer every year. At the tip of each twig is a bud. Leaves and a new shoot will sprout from this. New buds form on each twig at the end of the growing season, ready for next year.

Leaves

Leaves come in all shapes and sizes. They take in sunlight and change it into energy. The tree uses this energy to make its food. This process is called photosynthesis.

Deciduous
Copper Beech
Horse Chestnut
Sycamore
Oak

Conifers

Sitka Spruce

Chile Pine

Deciduous leaves can be made of a single piece or several lengths. Conifers usually keep their leaves through the winter. Coniferous leaves can be needle-shaped.

Flowers and fruit

All trees have flowers except conifers. Some are small and dull, but others are big and bright. The flower's job is to produce fruits. These fruits contain the seeds which will grow into new trees.

Elder   Orange

Mountain Ash berries

Wild Cherry   **Horse Chestnut**

Sowing the seed

Every apple core has several pips or seeds which can grow into a tree.

Even the biggest tree grows from a small seed. When it is old enough, it will grow seeds of its own. These are scattered in many ways. Some are blown by the wind. Others are carried away by birds and animals.

Seeds are scattered by the wind.

Many animals spread seeds around.

Seedlings

A seed lies in the soil all winter. In Spring it begins to grow. First a root goes down into the soil. Then a shoot pushes up into the light.

A forest nursery

The shoot grows two leaves and a bud. These seed leaves contain a store of food to help the young plants grow. In time, the bud opens and the first true leaves form. The roots also begin to spread as a growing tree needs more water and minerals.

Life in a tree

A tree makes a good home. Many birds, insects and other animals can live there. Caterpillars and moths may live on the leaves. Squirrels scamper along the branches looking for things to eat. Birds and beetles feed on small wasps and mites that live on the bark and leaves.

Blackbird

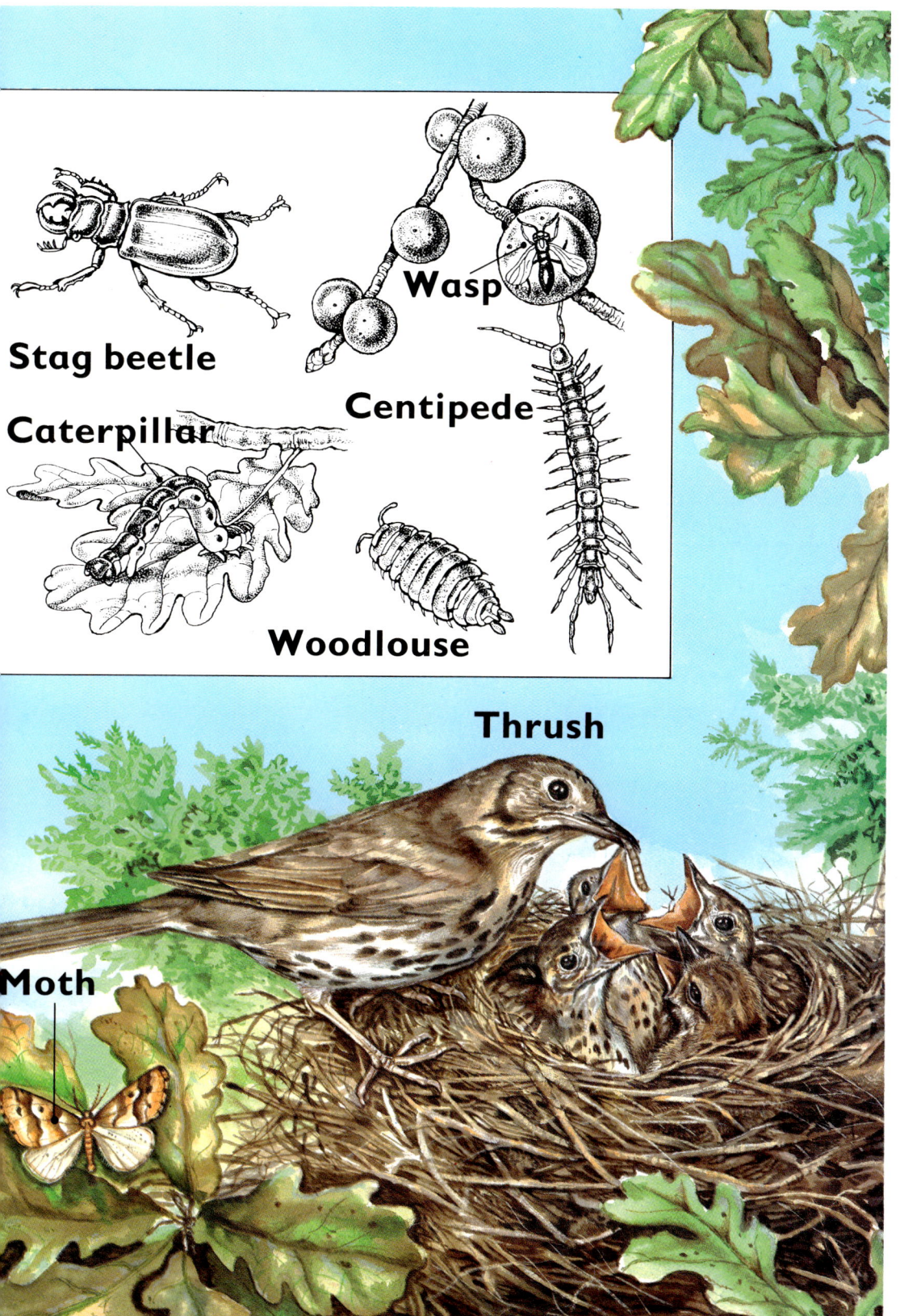

How old is it?

Trees can live longer than any other plant or animal. The bristlecone pine below was the oldest tree in the world. When it died it was almost 5,000 years old.

An elm killed by Dutch elm disease

A tree uprooted in a storm

Like all living things trees die when they grow old. A birch tree usually lives for about 60 years. They can also be killed by disease, fire or bad weather.

Forestry

Millions of trees are cut down every year. Trees must be planted all the time or there would be a shortage of timber. Here are some of the most popular woods.

Much of the timber we use is grown in large man-made forests. The trees grown are mostly conifers. These grow quickly and have long, straight trunks. This makes them easy to saw into planks. They are cut down with power saws.

Fire!

Forests can catch fire very easily. Once a fire starts, it is difficult to put out. Vast areas of forest are destroyed by fire every year. One way to fight a forest fire is to bomb burning areas with water.

Forests take many years to recover from a fire. So when you visit a forest, always follow the forest code.

The many uses of wood

Look around your home. You will see wood used in many ways. Floor boards, doors and chairs may all be made of wood. It is also used to make paper and cardboard. Some trees are grown for their fruit and others for their oil and bark.

Tree facts

The biggest living thing in the world is a Giant Sequoia tree in California. It is known as General Sherman and it weighs over 6,000 tonnes.

The tallest tree ever found was a Douglas fir in Canada. This giant, 126 m (415 ft) high, was cut down in 1902.

The tallest tree still standing is a Mountain Ash in Tasmania. This is 99 m (325 ft) high and still growing.

The heaviest timber in the world comes from the Black Ironwood tree which grows in South Africa.

The strange 'Dynamite' tree grows in Mexico. It bears fruits as big as oranges. When they are ripe, they explode! Luckily, this dangerous tree is rare.

The Banyan tree of India has roots which grow out of its trunk and branches. This makes it look as though it is upside down.

In the world every year, an area of forest as big as Great Britain is cut down.

The biggest forest is in the north of the USSR. It stretches over 1,100 million hectares (2,700 million acres).

Glossary

Here is the meaning of some of the words used in this book.

Broadleaved trees
Trees with wide flat leaves which grow in the warmer areas of the world.

Conifer
One of the two main tree groups. Conifers usually keep their leaves in winter.

Crown
The upper part of the tree – the branches and leaves.

Deciduous trees
Trees whose leaves die and drop off in Autumn. They grow new leaves in Spring.

Evergreen trees
Trees which keep their leaves all year round.

Minerals
Substances which are found naturally in the ground and which a tree needs to grow.

Roots
The part of the tree which is underground and takes up water from the soil.

Photosynthesis
The process by which plants turn light and air into energy to help them grow.

Sap
The watery fluid which carries food about a tree.

Trunks
The thick stem of the tree from which the branches grow.

Index

Bark 20, 28
Bird 20
Branch 6, 10, 11, 20, 31
Bud 11, 19

Cardboard 28
Caterpillar 20
Chair 28
Conifer 4, 14, 25, 31
Crown 6, 31

Deciduous tree 31
Deserts 4

Energy 12, 31
Evergreen tree 31

Fire 26, 27
Flower 14
Forest 25, 26, 27
Forest Code 27
Fruit 28

Heartwood 8

Insect 20

Leaves 6, 8, 11, 12, 19, 20

Minerals 10, 19, 31

Paper 28
Photosynthesis 12, 31
Pine 22

Roots 6, 10, 18, 19, 31

Sap 8, 31
Saw 25
Scar 11
Seeds 14, 16, 18, 19
Shoot 18, 29
Soil 6, 18, 31
Squirrel 20
Sunlight 12

Trunk 6, 8, 25, 31

Water 10, 19, 26
Wood 6, 25, 28

582.16 Langley, Andrew
LAN   Trees

$10.90   22271

DATE			

DISCARD

© THE BAKER & TAYLOR CO.